PATTERNS OF CHANGE
Student Literature

Center for Gifted Education
School of Education
The College of William and Mary

W&M
Center for
Gifted
Education

Unit Developer: Mary Pleiss

KENDALL/HUNT PUBLISHING COMPANY
4050 Westmark Drive   Dubuque, Iowa 52002

Book Team

Chairman and Chief Executive Officer: Mark C. Falb
Vice President, Director of National Book Program: Alfred C. Grisanti
Editorial Development Supervisor: Georgia Botsford
Developmental Editor: Angela Willenbring
Prepress Project Coordinator: Sheri Hosek
Prepress Editor: Carrie Maro
Permissions Editor: Colleen Zelinsky
Design Manager: Jodi Splinter

Author Information for Correspondence and Workshops:

Center for Gifted Education
The College of William and Mary
P.O. Box 8795
Williamsburg, VA 23187-8795
Phone: 757-221-2362
Email address: cfge@wm.edu
Web address: www.cfge.wm.edu

ISBN 978-0-7872-9395-6

Printed in the United States of America
10   9   8   7

CONTENTS

New feet within my garden go

Emily Dickinson

New feet within my garden go,
New fingers stir the sod;
A troubadour upon the elm
Betrays the solitude.

New children play upon the green,
New weary sleep below;
And still the pensive spring returns,
And still the punctual snow!

On the Pulse of Morning

Maya Angelou

Each new hour holds new chances
For a new beginning.
Do not be wedded forever
To fear, yoked eternally
To brutishness.

The horizon leans forward,
Offering you space
To place new steps of change
Here, on the pulse of this fine day
You may have the courage
To look up and out and upon me,
The Rock, the River, the Tree, your country.
No less to Midas than the mendicant.
No less to you now than the mastodon then.

Here, on the pulse of this new day
You may have the grace to look up and out
And into your sister's eyes,
And into your brother's face,
Your country,
And say simply
Very simply
With hope—
Good morning.

The Helpful Badger

retold by Laurence Yep

Once in Japan, there was a man named Kitabayashi. On the day that his son got married, he invited family, friends, and neighbors to a feast. There were all sorts of good things to eat, but the man made sure everyone ate some *sekiban*—a special dish of rice and red beans that was thought to bring good luck.

The guests were having such a good time that the party went on late into the night. Although there had been many people, there was still a great deal of food left over.

When the last guest had gone, Mr. Kitabayashi yawned. "It is late," he said to his wife. "Let's put everything away in the morning."

Relieved, the couple left everything where it was and went to bed. Around midnight, Mr. Kitabayashi was awakened by a noise. As he lay on his mat, he heard another thump from the next room.

Quietly, he got up and crept out into the hallway. From within the room, he heard thumps and bumps. Is it thieves? he asked himself, suddenly afraid. Slowly, he slid back a screen door and peeked inside the room.

Roaming over the floor mats were twelve creatures. Some were young; others were gray-backed elders. They waddled about on their short, stubby legs, sniffing at this or that. "Badgers! I wonder how they got in," he muttered to himself, then went to get a broom to chase them out.

When he returned, he found them all gathered around a bowl of *sekiban*. The younger ones tried to thrust their muzzles in, but the older ones rapped them sharply. Then, while the younger ones watched, the elders dipped their paws in and scooped out handfuls of *sekiban*, careful not to drop any on the floor. Mr. Kitabayashi chuckled to himself. "It's almost as if the parents are teaching the young ones manners."

Tickled, he watched the badgers eat hungrily. He noticed how thin they all looked. "Times must be hard, eh?" he whispered. "Poor badgers. Are you having trouble finding enough to eat? You must be, or why would you sneak in here?" He thought for a moment and then smiled. "I've known what it's like to be hungry. I will share our good fortune with you, for this has been a happy day."

Sliding the door shut, the kindly man put away the broom and went back to bed. "What was that noise?" his wife asked.

"Just a few guests," Mr. Kitabayashi said. "They arrived late."

"They've got some nerve," the wife said. "Did you tell them to go home?"

Mr. Kitabayashi thought of the badger family. "They'll leave soon. They've kept on their coats."

"How rude," his wife complained.

"They're not so bad," he replied. "Let's not spoil their fun." He rolled over.

However, his wife nudged him. "Well, who are they?"

"Mr. and Mrs. Badger," he mumbled sleepily.

"Badgers! In my house! They'll make a mess of everything," Mrs. Kitabayashi said, poking him urgently. "Go chase them away."

But after twenty years of marriage, Mr. Kitabayashi's back was like iron to his wife's elbow. "Not these badgers. They're very well behaved." Mr. Kitabayashi went back to sleep.

"If you aren't the oddest man," his wife said with a sigh, but she was so tired from the day that she fell asleep, too.

The next morning, the mess was exactly as they had left it—though the *sekiban* bowl had been licked completely clean. "You see," Mr. Kitabayashi said cheerfully, "I told you the badgers were polite guests."

After they had cleaned up the house, Mr. Kitabayashi went looking for a hole in the wall. When he found it, he covered it up carefully. But all the rest of the day, he felt guilty. "I wonder if the little ones are getting enough to eat?" So that evening after supper, he put out some of the left-overs outside their house.

His wife watched him, mystified. "Aren't you the strangest man? Why are you doing that?"

"It's for last night's guests," Mr. Kitabayashi said, and he told her about what he had seen.

His wife was not sure that it was such a good idea. "You'll just encourage them to come back. Badgers can be pretty rowdy animals."

"Not these badgers," Mr. Kitabayashi insisted. "They have good manners."

Since her husband was set on putting out food, Mrs. Kitabayashi stopped arguing.

The next day, all the food was gone. Mr. Kitabayashi held up the empty bowl. "You see, they did come."

"Humph, we're probably just feeding some stray cat," his wife mumbled. But that night, she let him set out more leftovers. She would have gone to bed, but Mr. Kitabayashi wanted her to stay up and see whether they came again.

"You're getting odder and odder," Mrs. Kitabayashi said in exasperation.

Her husband held onto her hand. "Perhaps, but sit with me awhile. There will be a full moon tonight. Remember how we used to sit and watch it?"

"For old time's sake, then." She pretended to grumble, but she wanted to keep an eye out inside their house.

Sure enough, as the moon rose, they watched the badgers trot toward the house with their peculiar gait. Their powerful, broad backs seemed to roll up and down. In the moonlight, their fur shone all silvery.

When the badgers encircled the bowl, they began to dip their paws in politely. "You see, it is just like I said." Mr. Kitabayashi nudged his wife.

"They're so cute," she replied.

From then on, they left food out every night. Sometimes, Mrs. Kitabayashi even made special treats for the badger family.

Then one night, Mr. Kitabayashi heard a thump inside his house. Believing that the badgers had returned, he blinked sleepily. That's gratitude for you, he thought. They've broken into our house again.

As he started to get up to scold them, the bedroom door slid to the side. Two tall shadowy figures stood in the doorway. These were no badgers.

"W-w-who are you?" stammered Mr. Kitabayashi.

Shutting the door behind them, they padded noiselessly into the room. In the moonlight, Mr. Kitabayashi saw two men. A sword blade flashed as one man drew it out. "Tell us where you have your money," the swordsman demanded.

Mr. Kitabayashi hid under the comforter and clung to his wife. "I-I-I have no money in the house."

The thief held the sword next to his throat. "Don't lie, or we'll kill you."

Suddenly, there was a loud noise in the house. The thieves straightened and turned. "What's that?" one of them asked just as the bedroom door crashed down.

Two huge wrestlers stood in the doorway. They looked as solid as boulders with legs. One wrestler pointed toward the street for the thieves to go. Then he lifted his large hands and flexed the fingers menacingly—the robbers would face those hands if they stayed.

"You can't scare me while I have this." The swordsman raised his blade above his head and brought it down in a wicked slash. But as large as the wrestler was, he was also lightning-quick. Leaping nimbly to the side, he caught the swords-man's wrist.

With a flip and a twist, he turned the swords-man head over heels until the thief was flat on his back. Then the wrestler adjusted his grip and tightened it until the swordsman cried out in pain. When the sword clattered to the floor, the wrestler kicked it over to his partner, who picked it up.

Turning, the first wrestler glowered at the other thief. Again he pointed toward the street. Then he stamped his foot so hard that the house seemed to shake.

"Yes, whatever you say," the second thief babbled, and he helped his moaning companion to his feet. Then they dashed out of the house and were never seen again.

"You have our eternal gratitude," Mr. Kitabayashi said. He and his wife got to their knees and bowed thankfully until their foreheads touched the floor. When they straightened up, the wrestlers had vanished.

"How could anyone so big be so quiet?" Mrs. Kitabayashi asked. They looked all around the house and then out at the street, but there was no sign of their rescuers.

"Who could it be?" Mr. Kitabayashi asked his wife.

"It must have been someone magical," his wife said. "But who?"

Although they sat up for a while, trying to figure out who had rescued them, it was still a mystery. Finally, when they were both so exhausted they could not keep their eyes open, they went to sleep.

Mr. Kitabayashi dreamed that he and his wife were sitting in their guest room in their best clothes. Then the screen door slid back and in waddled one badger after another; until they had formed a row in front of them.

At last, the largest and oldest badger stepped forward and bowed its head. "We cannot express our gratitude when you are awake. So we come in this dream to thank you. Food has been scarce of late. Without your generosity, we would have starved."

Mr. Kitabayashi was embarrassed for thinking of such intelligent creatures as pets. "Think nothing of it."

The badger raised a paw. "We would be beasts if we weren't grateful. That is why we came to your rescue."

"So it was *you* who saved us," Mr. Kitabayashi cried in delight.

"We can take many forms," the badger told him. "From now on, rest easy at night, for one of us will always be guarding you."

"And you will never go hungry," Mr. Kitabayashi promised.

"Now, in your honor, my daughters will dance," the badger said, and he sat up on his haunches. As he took a breath, his belly suddenly swelled up, and softly he began to beat time on his stomach. *"Teketen-teketen-teketen."* Then the mother joined in. *"Dokodon-dokodon-dokodon."*

One of the young ones rose on her hind legs. "We wish your family well," she said sweetly, and she did a little dance like one of the wedding guests had done. She set her hind paws down with delicate pats on the floor mats, her claws clicking in time to the drumbeat. *"Pom-poko pom."* She began to sing. *"Pom-poko pom."*

Another youngster leapt up and joined in. The Kitabayashis watched, fascinated, until the dance had stopped. Then with another bow, the badgers waddled out.

The next morning, Mr. Kitabayashi could not wait to tell his wife. "I just had the oddest dream." And he told her about the badgers' visit.

"Your oddness must be catching," his wife said, "because I dreamed the same thing."

That night, and every night after that, the Kitabayashis left food for the badgers. Sometimes they saw a peculiar, large rock by their front door that had not been there during the day and was gone the next morning. Then they would leave a cup of tea, for they knew it was a badger bodyguard.

all ignorance toboggans into know

e.e. cummings

all ignorance toboggans into know
and trudges up to ignorance again:
but winter's not forever,even snow
melts;and if spring should spoil the game,what then?

all history's a winter sport or three:
but were it five,i'd still insist that all
history is too small for even me;
for me and you,exceedingly too small.

Swoop(shrill collective myth)into thy grave
merely to toil the scale to shrillerness
per every madge and mabel dick and dave
—tomorrow is our permanent address

and there they'll scarcely find us(if they do,
we'll move away still further:into now

In the Windowsill

Mary Pleiss

Red geraniums grow in the windowsill
Night comes and they close like fans
Scented sharp and green, their crushed leaves
Perfuming the room with their own spring

Night comes, and they close like fans
The faces of children, softened by dreams
Perfuming the room with their own spring
Mud and clover and dandelion greens

The faces of children, softened by dreams
Blending their days and memories
Mud and clover and dandelion greens
Melting together in sleep and dark

Blending their days and memories
Scented sharp and green, their crushed leaves
Melting together in sleep and dark
Red geraniums grow in the windowsill

Frequently the woods are pink

Emily Dickinson

Frequently the woods are pink,
Frequently are brown;
Frequently the hills undress
Behind my native town.

Oft a head is crested
I was wont to see,
And as oft a cranny
Where it used to be.

And the earth, they tell me,
On its axis turned,—
Wonderful rotation
By but twelve performed!

As children bid the guest good-night

Emily Dickinson

As children bid the guest good-night,
And then reluctant turn,
My flowers raise their pretty lips,
Then put their nightgowns on.

As children caper when they wake,
Merry that it is morn,
My flowers from a hundred cribs
Will peep, and prance again.

The Wind Is Blowing West

Joseph Ceravolo

1
I am trying to decide to go swimming,
But the sea looks so calm.
All the other boys have gone in.
I can't decide what to do.

I've been waiting in my tent
Expecting to go in.
Have you forgotten to come down?
Can I escape going in?
I was just coming

I was just going in
But lost my pail

2
A boisterous tide is coming up;
I was just looking at it.
The pail is near me
again. My shoulders have sand on them.

Round the edge of the tide
Is the shore. The shore
Is filled with waves.
They are tin waves.

Boisterous tide coming up.
The tide is getting less.

3
Daytime is not a brain,
Living is not a cricket's song.
Why does light diffuse
As earth turns away from the sun?

I want to give my food
To a stranger. I want
to be taken.
What kind of a face do

I have while leaving?
I'm thinking of my friend.

4
I am trying to go swimming
But the sea looks so calm
All boys are gone
I can't decide what to do

I've been waiting to go
Have you come down?
Can I escape

I am just coming
    Just going in

A Bouquet of Wild Flowers

Laura Ingalls Wilder

The Man of the Place brought me a bouquet of wild flowers this morning. It has been a habit of his for years. He never brings me cultivated flowers but always the wild blossoms of field and woodland, and I think them much more beautiful.

In my bouquet this morning was a purple flag. Do you remember gathering them down on the flats and in the creek bottoms when you were a barefoot child? There was one marshy corner of the pasture down by the creek, where the grass grew lush and green; where the cows loved to feed and could always be found when it was time to drive them up at night. All thru the tall grass were scattered purple and white flag blossoms and I have stood in that peaceful grassland corner, with the red cow and the spotted cow and the roan taking their goodnight mouthfuls of the sweet grass, and watched the sun setting behind the hilltop and loved the purple flags and the rippling brook and wondered at the beauty of the world, while I wriggled my bare toes down into the soft grass.

The wild Sweet Williams in my bouquet brought a far different picture to my mind. A window had been broken in the schoolhouse at the country crossroads and the pieces of glass lay scattered where they had fallen. Several little girls going to school for their first term had picked handfuls of Sweet Williams and were gathered near the window. Someone discovered that the blossoms could be pulled from the stem and, by wetting their faces, could be stuck to the pieces of glass in whatever fashion they were arranged. They dried on the glass and would stay that way for hours and, looked at thru the glass, were very pretty. I was one of those little girls and tho I have forgotten what it was that I tried to learn out of a book that summer, I never have forgotten the beautiful wreaths and stars and other figures we made on the glass with the Sweet Williams. The delicate fragrance of their blossoms this morning made me feel like a little girl again.

The little white daisies with their hearts of gold grew thickly along the path where we walked to Sunday school. Father and sister and I used to walk the 2¹/₂ miles every Sunday morning. The horses had worked hard all the week and must rest this one day, and Mother would rather stay at home with baby brother, so with Father and Sister Mary I walked to the church thru the beauties of the sunny spring Sundays. I have forgotten what I was taught on those days also. I was only a little girl, you know. But I can still plainly see the grass and the trees and the path winding ahead, flecked with sunshine and shadow and the beautiful golden-hearted daisies scattered all along the way.

Ah well! That was years ago and there have been so many changes since then that it would seem such simple things should be forgotten, but at the long last, I am beginning to learn that it is the sweet, simple things of life which are the real ones after all.

We heap up around us things that we do not need as the crow makes piles of glittering pebbles. We gabble words like parrots until we lose the sense of their meaning; we chase after this new idea and that; we take an old thought and dress it out in so many words that the thought itself is lost in its clothing like a slim woman in a barrel skirt and then we exclaim, "Lo, the wonderful new thought I have found!"

"There is nothing new under the sun," says the proverb. I think the meaning is that there are just so many truths or laws of life and no matter how far we may think we have advanced we cannot get

---

Originally appeared in the *Missouri Realist*, July 20, 1917.

beyond those laws. However complex a structure we build of living we must come back to those truths and so we find we have traveled in a circle.

The Russian revolution has only taken the Russian people back to the democratic form of government they had at the beginning of history in medieval times and so a republic is nothing new. I believe we would be happier to have a personal revolution in our individual lives and go back to simpler living and more direct thinking. It is the simple things of life that make living worth while, the sweet fundamental things such as love and duty, work and rest and living close to nature. There are no hothouse blossoms that can compare in beauty and fragrance with my bouquet of wild flowers.

Below

Joseph Bruchac

A Hopi friend
once told me that the people came
from another world beneath this world.
Before that world,
they lived in another and
another one still, so that the world
we live in today is the fourth one
the people have known.

Each time, it seems,
things were going well,
until something happened
that made things go wrong.
People acted jealous,
people fought one another.
People didn't remember to respect the sacred.
Coyote caused the greatest trouble,
when he stole the child of the water monster.
When the water monster took back its child,
the whole third world was washed over by flood.

So the people left their old world behind.
They had to climb higher
to another, safer place.

Perhaps that great canyon
in the heart of their lands
was meant to remind us
of those worlds that were lost
before we reached this rainbow world
no one wants to leave behind.

Buffalo Dusk

Carl Sandburg

The buffaloes are gone.
And those who saw the buffaloes are gone.
Those who saw the buffaloes by thousands and how they pawed the
  prairie sod into dust with their hoofs, their great heads down
  pawing on in a great pageant of dusk,
Those who saw the buffaloes are gone.
And the buffaloes are gone.

From *Smoke and Steel*, 1920, Harcourt Brace.

Walking

Linda Hogan

It began in dark and underground weather, a slow hunger moving toward light. It grew in a dry gully beside the road where I live, a place where entire hillsides are sometimes yellow, windblown tides of sunflower plants. But this one was different. It was alone, and larger than the countless others who had established their lives further up the hill. This one was a traveler, a settler, and like a dream beginning in conflict, it grew where the land had been disturbed.

I saw it first in early summer. It was a green and sleeping bud, raising itself toward the sun. Ants worked around the unopened bloom, gathering aphids and sap. A few days later, it was a tender young flower, soft and new, with a pale green center and a troop of silver gray insects climbing up and down the stalk.

Over the summer this sunflower grew into a plant of incredible beauty, turning its face daily toward the sun in the most subtle of ways, the black center of it dark and alive with a deep blue light, as if flint had sparked an elemental fire there, in community with rain, mineral, mountain air, and sand.

As summer changed from green to yellow there were new visitors daily: the lace-winged insects, the bees whose legs were fat with pollen, and grasshoppers with their clattering wings and desperate hunger. There were other lives I missed, lives too small or hidden to see. It was as if this plant with its host of lives was a society, one in which moment by moment, depending on light and moisture, there was great and diverse change.

There were changes in the next larger world around the plant as well. One day I rounded a bend in the road to find the disturbing sight of a dead horse, black and still against a hillside, eyes rolled back. Another day I was nearly lifted by a wind and sandstorm so fierce and hot that I had to wait for it to pass before I could return home. On this day the faded dry petals of the sunflower were swept across the land. That was when the birds arrived to carry the new seeds to another future.

In this one plant, in one summer season, a drama of need and survival took place. Hungers were filled. Insects coupled. There was escape, exhaustion, and death. Lives touched down a moment and were gone.

I was an outsider. I only watched. I never learned the sunflower's golden language or the tongues of its citizens. I had a small understanding, nothing more than a shallow observation of the flower, insects, and birds. But they knew what to do, how to live. An old voice from somewhere, gene or cell, told the plant how to evade the pull of gravity and find its way upward, how to open. It was instinct, intuition, necessity. A certain knowing directed the seedbearing birds on paths to ancestral homelands they had never seen. They believed it. They followed.

There are other summons and calls, some even more mysterious than those commandments to birds or those survival journeys of insects. In bamboo plants, for instance, with their thin green canopy of light and golden stalks that creak in the wind. Once a century, all of a certain kind of bamboo flower on the same day. Whether they are in Malaysia or in a greenhouse in Minnesota makes no difference, nor does the age or size of the plant. They flower. Some current of an inner language passes between them, through space and separation, in ways we cannot explain in our language. They are all, somehow, one plant, each with a share of communal knowledge.

Reprinted from *Parabola, The Magazine of Myth and Tradition*, Volume XV, No. 2, Supper, 1990, with permission of the author.

John Hay, in *The Immortal Wilderness*, has written: "There are occasions when you can hear the mysterious language of the Earth, in water, or coming through the trees, emanating from the mosses, seeping through the undercurrents of the soil, but you have to be willing to wait and receive."

Sometimes I hear it talking. The light of the sunflower was one language, but there are others, more audible. Once, in the redwood forest, I heard a beat, something like a drum or heart coming from the ground and trees and wind. That underground current stirred a kind of knowing inside me, a kinship and longing, a dream barely remembered that disappeared back to the body.

Another time, there was the booming voice of an ocean storm thundering from far out at sea, telling about what lived in the distance, about the rough water that would arrive, wave after wave revealing the disturbance at the center.

Tonight I walk. I am watching the sky. I think of the people who came before me and how they knew the placement of stars in the sky, watched the moving sun long and hard enough to witness how a certain angle of light touched a stone only once a year. Without written records, they knew the gods of every night, the small, fine details of the world around them and of immensity above them.

Walking, I can almost hear the redwoods beating. And the oceans are above me here, rolling clouds, heavy and dark, considering snow. On the dry, red road, I pass the place of the sunflower, that dark and secret location where creation took place. I wonder if it will return this summer, if it will multiply and move up to the other stand of flowers in a territorial struggle.

It's winter and there is smoke from the fires. The square, lighted windows of houses are fogging over. It is a world of elemental attention, of all things working together, listening to what speaks in the blood. Whichever road I follow, I walk in the land of many gods, and they love and eat one another.

Walking, I am listening to a deeper way. Suddenly all my ancestors are behind me. Be still, they say. Watch and listen. You are the result of the love of thousands.

When forty winters shall beseige thy brow

William Shakespeare

When forty winters shall beseige thy brow,
And dig deep trenches in thy beauty's field,
Thy youth's proud livery, so gazed on now,
Will be a tatter'd weed, of small worth held:
Then being ask'd where all thy beauty lies,
Where all the treasure of thy lusty days,
To say, within thine own deep-sunken eyes,
Were an all-eating shame and thriftless praise.
How much more praise deserved thy beauty's use,
If thou couldst answer 'This fair child of mine
Shall sum my count and make my old excuse,'
Proving his beauty by succession thine!
This were to be new made when thou art old,
And see thy blood warm when thou feel'st it cold.

from Little Gidding

T. S. Eliot

What we call the beginning is often the end
And to make an end is to make a beginning.
The end is where we start from. And every phrase . . .

Every phrase and every sentence is an end and a beginning,
Every poem an epitaph . . .

A people without history
Is not redeemed from time, for history is a pattern
Of timeless moments. So, while the light fails
On a winter's afternoon, in a secluded chapel
History is now and England.

With the drawing of this Love and the voice of this Calling

We shall not cease from exploration
And the end of all our exploring
Will be to arrive where we started
And know the place for the first time.